Praise for How to Create a Real Estate Money Machine and Retire with Income

"As Managing Director of one of the world's leading market forecasting firms, I have a lot of experience analyzing liquid markets such as Stocks, Bonds, Commodities, and Currencies. When I am asked about Real Estate, I have my "Go To" person: Michael Douville. He has a unique ability to help frame a proper mindset and appreciation for Real Estate as a portion of a portfolio.

David Gurwitz JD, MBA, CPA
Managing Director: Charles Nenner Research

If you dream of a basic strategy that will create steady income to last a life time. If you are willing to adopt a simple and long term plan to become wealthy and have the freedom of spending your time doing things you love to do.If you want the plan from someone who has "been there, done that'? THEN THIS IS THE BOOK FOR YOU. Michael Douville shares the plan that worked for him and created a reliable income for life. This comes from a real man with real results and now he is willing to share just how he did it. Michael's plan is one that worked for me, and it will work for you, too.

John Foltz
Investor, Motivational Speaker, Philanthropist
Past President of the Arizona Association of Realtors
Past Chairman of National Association of Realtors Strategic Planning

Investment theories are everywhere and usually are just that, theory. Michael Douville's "How to Create a Real Estate Money Machine and Retire with Income" is based on actual experience. He shows real life examples, what to look for, how to analyze a potential property, how to find a property manager and real estate professional, basically, everything he has learned in 40+ years of successful real estate investing that will result in your cash flow creation and personal freedom. I have personally implemented Michael's approach and can tell you that I have a big smile every month when I receive my rent checks!

If you want freedom, a positive cash flow is a great way of achieving it!

Joe Needham, MBA

If you are an investor looking for retirement income, why risk the stock market? Every 7-8 years there is a crash that would seriously impact your retirement income - 2000- 2008. Everyone needs a place to live and rentals will always be there. Also, the many tax advantages using real estate as an income stream.

Lt. John Rowton Chicago Police Dept. Ret.

"The strategy of using rental units as an integral part of a solid retirement plan is not a new one but is commonly overlooked or not even considered by serious individuals or advisors. This book is a masterful, hands-on, practical guide to incorporating rentals that can equal or exceed your returns on all other investments. It is a must read for anyone whether for pure investment purposes only or those who are preparing for their journey towards a rewarding retirement."

Joseph Paonessa,

Attorney; President and Founder of America's MortgageBanc Corp. Former President of the National Association of Mortgage Brokers Past President of the Arizona Association of Mortgage Professionals

I found your book to be well presented and as understandable as the ABC"s. I strongly recommend the concepts for anyone looking for a cookbook with recipes to follow for investments and careers. The examples say it all.

Dr. Melvyn N. Zobler

HOW TO
CREATE A REAL ESTATE
MONEY
MACHINE
AND RETIRE WITH INCOME

Michael Douville

I wish to thank my wife for all she has done for me over these 36 years. She has taught me the meaning of Family, which is Forever.

I wish to thank my sons Ryan and Rob for their encouragement and insight.

As way to begin, I have had an absolutely incredible Life! My intention is to inspire others to break away from the mundane and follow your dreams. For me, Family is Forever! The Strategy to accumulate Wealth and more importantly Income has allowed me to be present at every Teacher Conference, every Band recital, every Boy Scout meeting, every Camp out, every fishing trip, every school event, every Birthday, every Graduation. I have been a Basketball Coach, Football Coach, Adult Boy Scout leader, and been involved on every level of my family. My wife and I have taken our children throughout the South Pacific and have spent late May, June, July, and early August in Burleigh Heads, Queensland, Australia for almost 20 years on the beach and in the water. In short, the Strategy we employed has given us Freedom; the Strategy will give **you freedom as well.**

Table of Contents

INTRODUCTION

W ealth! What is it? How do you get it? There are no courses taught in school that teach students how to obtain wealth and yet hundreds of books are written about it! Everyone wants it and people have died in its pursuit. Wealth is elusive yet we all know who the wealthy are – or do we?

Webster's Dictionary defines wealth as "much money or property; riches." Most people think of the wealthy as the super-rich such as Bill Gates, Warren Buffet, or Donald Trump, but if we dig deeper, there are many wealthy people who live quiet fulfilling lives secure in the fact that their assets protect them from some of life's problems. Wealth allows for problems to be split: those that can be solved with money become Expenses, those that cannot be solved with money are real Problems. These wealthy individuals are able to follow their dreams and contribute their time and talents to family and friends and to the benefit of society in general. The wealthy are free of the time commitment necessary to provide the essentials of life because their wealth frees them from the necessity of a job or a job they do not enjoy! This is the type of true wealth that we will define and outline a strategy to achieve.

Wealth, as I define it, is the ability to maintain our lifestyle unaffected by change in the economic environment such as recession, interest rate increase or decrease, inflation or deflation, loss of job due to downsizing or government regulations, or change in your family's health. My type of wealth provides incredible security and opportunity for your family. It allows for extended travel to far-off and exotic destinations, allowing yourself and family to experience other cultures and visit our earth's natural beauty.

1

Wealth will allow your children or grandchildren to be better educated, better clothed and fed, and they can go to summer camp, or learn to play golf and tennis. All provided by wealth!

My wealth strategy has allowed me to write part of this book in the South Pacific where I traveled for four months. I wrote parts of this book in Fiji, across Australia, and in a new luxury eighth floor condo overlooking the Pacific in Mt. Manganui, New Zealand. I was able to travel where I desired for as long as I wished because I had formulated a wealth building strategy which I will outline later on, and then put into action. My book is designed so you can follow in my footsteps and succeed! You can achieve as great a wealth as you desire! You can build wealth that will pay all your expenses, give you play money, and still grow each and every month! Getting started and changing one's lifestyle and habits is the greatest challenge, cutting expenses and building reserves is not easy and requires total commitment by all parties involved and the first few years <u>are</u> the toughest, but if you follow my guide, <u>you will succeed!</u>

Different Asset Classes

There are different assets that vary the forms of wealth. One milestone for Wealth commonly used is the accumulation of one million dollars, in one of these forms: cash, stock, bonds, or real estate. There are of course other forms such as art, jewelry, collectibles such as stamps and coins, or intellectual properties, but the above four asset classes are by far the most common. I do not profess to be an economic professor, but I do have a working understanding of these basic classes.

Cash is an excellent form of wealth! Cash can be used for everything, plus it is easily transferred and is understood by everyone. Obtaining One Million Dollars (U.S. currency) will open the door for many opportunities and lots of luxuries. Ask a lottery winner about their winnings – you can buy a house, a car, a vacation, etc, etc. But after you have spent the money – IT IS GONE! FOREVER! Cash in and of itself generates no Income.

One needs a place to live, if you purchase a $450,000 house, you can pay cash or borrow! Let's borrow $360,000 with $90,000 down (20%), that translates into 360K @ 4.5% = $1824.00 per month Principal & Interest but we also have taxes of $150/month and insurance of $40/month for a house payment of approx $2014/month. Let's buy a car – cash or credit? Let's finance as most people do and let's not go overboard, but let's lease a $30K car at $299/ month (a very good deal!) over 3 years plus insurance of at least $100/month. So we have bought a car and a house, we need utilities $250/month, health insurance $650/mo., food and entertainment $800/month, you know your kids are going to want clothes and computer games $300/month, you will want cable

3

$50/month, a gardener $100/month, cell phones $100/month, internet access $60/month, health club $90/month, probably a second car – used $250/month, plus $100/insurance, gas and maintenance $300/month, and let's go on a 2 week family vacation – fly/drive at $5000 or $416/month for a monthly obligation of $5250 per month; have we forgotten anything? YES! The IRS will want at least $6000 a year or $500/month to bring our total to $6379/month. There is probably more, but a target of $6500 will suffice.

Spending approximately $6500 every month is a very good estimate of how most middle-class Americans live in the 2000's. Following my $1 million in cash example and financing the purchase of the houses and cars to preserve the funds, there would be about $910,000 left. If it stays in cash, I have 910,000/6,5 00= 140 months of payments before our cash is <u>ALL GONE.</u> So I will probably will not leave my $Million in cash, but will seek other alternatives.

I can place the money in other asset classes: stocks, bonds, CD s, or Real Estate. With conservative stocks, the dividends generally are well less than 3% annually ($27,300) and although total returns have been in the double digits for the past several years, a Bear Market can completely erase years of gains. Studies further suggest that the average Investor earns much less than the average returns of the S&P due to caution and inexperience coupled with the average portfolios are usually not fully invested. Currently in 2015, risk is rising as a Global Slowdown is possible and in a Global Economy, problems do not necessarily need to START in the US to affect local US markets. Prudence would dictate that profits be taken and funds re-allocated to other asset classes that have not experienced such a rapid rise as the Stock and Bond Markets which many believe are unsustainable. The stocks that have had enormous returns generate extremely little if any income and necessitate the selling of the asset to pay for life's expenses and in so doing, we reduce the number of shares held. Further, each time there is a need for money, if there has been a gain, a tax liability is generated. I certainly do not advocate the complete avoidance of stock ownership, but as an income source it has its limitations. Ideally, the principal should grow or in the least, remain unused and the earnings derived from the investment can be spent.

A great source of income are debt instruments such as Ginnie Mae's (Government National Mortgage Association) which is a fund of loans issued mainly by FHA and VA to fund single family and multi-family homes and insured by government agencies, bond funds (Government, Corporate, and High-Yield), MLP's (Master Limited Partnerships), CD's etc. Each of these instruments generate cash streams that are dependable, consistent, and generally considered safe and conservative. Great safety of principal is historically achievable. The yields available are commensurate with the risk of the investment vehicle but a conservative mix will yield 2-3% annually in 2015. We have $910K, if we invest at 3% we receive $27,300 a year without reducing our $910K. We can receive that amount forever! We estimated our monthly obligations of between $6-6,500/month and this debt instrument income amount is $2275/month. A shortage of $3300 a month. Rates are currently very low and at some time they will rise; the Principal, however, will decline. These are Fixed Income Investments and there is no growth of Income. The $910,000 can subsidize the shortage for 275 months, a very long time, but the Nest Egg is declining each and every month. Further, as rates rise, the value of the fixed income will decline further eroding the Principal, just a 2% rise in long term rates can devastate a Fixed Income Portfolio.

A short word about current Bond Market conditions. Rates around the world have been declining for almost 30 years and are historically low. The cycle has changed and rates will begin to rise over at least the next decade and perhaps beyond. Government Bonds are negative in Europe. Corporate Bonds are being issued by companies to position themselves for the future with extremely low rates and are loading the balance sheets with long term debt. High Yield Bonds were issued to domestic Oil Companies in enormous quantities to fund the **Oil Boom** which is now heading to the **Oil Bust**. Not only must one consider declining credit quality, as an Investor, one must consider the prospect of an eventual rise in rates. As rates increase, the value of the fixed instrument declines and it can decline DRAMATICALLY, very quickly. Rather than a lender, Investors should borrow all the long term fixed rate loans possible, exactly the same as most of the Fortune 500 companies are today. The forecast for Rising rates means rising prices. Hopefully oil will never be more than $56 a barrel and the cost of health care will never go up, and milk will always be less than $2.50 a gallon. We forgot about INFLATION!

Inflation, which is widely defined as rising costs and prices, is the cancer of a fixed income portfolio. Although the income amount is constant and consistent, the effect of this inflation will shrink the purchasing power considerably overtime. Consider a modest 2% inflation over just 5 years. 2% inflation IS very modest and the time frame I use is 10 – 30 years of post employment. The monthly expenses are $6500/month and I can fix the interest rate on my home so that is constant, but what about real estate taxes, insurance, water, phone, gas, electricity? I pay more now than I did five years ago, so will you! Here is a 2% impact in purchasing power over 5 years:

Year 0:	$65,000
Year 1:	$63,700
Year 2:	$62,426
Year 3:	$61,177
Year 4:	$59,953
Year 5:	$58,754

Inflation always wins! It will grind out the income and in 5 years $65000 of purchasing power will have eroded – by over 9.5% in 5 years of benign inflation! That loss will necessitate the use of the principal to maintain your lifestyle and over time it will be ALL GONE. You will DIE BROKE! As long as you are terminally ill and KNOW EXACTLY when you and your spouse will DIE, THAT IS JUST FINE! Fortunately people are living way beyond most expectations and statistically speaking, I have an extremely good likelihood of living well into my 80's, being active and healthy. There will be more people living past 100 than ever experienced in the history of the planet. I am planning to live to 100 and to live well to 100 years old. My Strategy must be Inflation sensitive, able to adjust to changing conditions and thrive!

Divergences

I have recommended a well diversified stock and bond portfolio with income and growth in the past as part of a Strategic Diversification. Dividends, interest payments, and capital gain distribution will all contribute to pay life's mundane expenses like mortgage payments, insurance, utilities, taxes, food etc. However, currently in 2015, the dividend yield is less than 2% which is not generous. There is the possibility of additional growth and with much more risk a 7-9% return could be achieved but stable and much less volatile assets are in the 2-4 % range with all of these assets negatively impacted by inflation. Further, Divergences are starting to appear in the Equity Markets as the S&P is heading to all time highs while the GDP is declining indicating possible trouble ahead. A dangerous divergence.

Currently, in the Spring of 2015, Global stock markets have also diverged from the underlying economics of the Global Gross Domestic Product or GDP which is currently estimated at less than 1%, however, the Stock markets continue to march to all-time highs. This graph Courtesy of Zerohedge is very enlightening:

"higher highs"

World MSCI
Stock Index

World GDP
Expectations 2014

"lower lows"

Dec   Mar   Jun   Sep   Dec   Mar   Jun
2012   2013   2014

This divergence shown by the graph is indicative of an aging Bull Market approaching "Bubble" proportions in both the Equity and Fixed Income Markets; perhaps as late as the Mania Phase. My strong advice is to take profits and re-allocate to Income Real Estate which is still in the beginning of a Bull market and probably in the Awareness Phase approaching the first correction which will again be a buying opportunity. The cycle for Real Estate is much longer and the Real Estate Crash of 2008 removed the Mal-investments restarting the cycle. Should the Equity Markets suffer significant declines, the correction in Real Estate could be of a higher magnitude, but it should be only a correction in an ongoing Bull Market. Several markets across the US will represent HUGE buying opportunities; Phoenix, Austin, Denver, Dallas-Ft. Worth, and Houston in particular. I strongly believe the Greatest Real Estate Bull Market in my lifetime is coming in the 2019 to 2025 time frame which may coincide with the Mania Phase. At that point, it may be time to take profits!

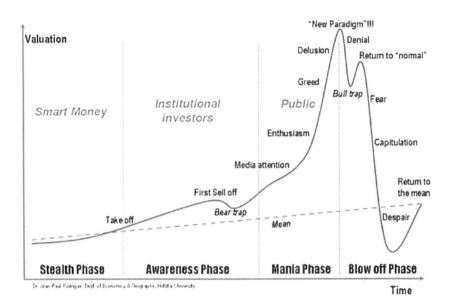

To be wealthy, I must accumulate assets which will not only retain their value, but also have excellent potential for growth in value and revenue generation. My overriding additional consideration is that the asset must also generate current cash flow. Cash flow pays the bills, cash flow pays for airline & cruise tickets, cash flow pays for cars and boats. Cash flow is <u>MAGIC!</u> My favorite asset class, which gives value stability and still grows while producing a high <u>monthly</u> yield, is real estate!

Residential Rentals

Residential Rental Real Estate is great for several economic reasons:

(1) Real Estate is a separate asset class and is not directly linked to the stock and bond markets and as such has much less volatility and is a great diversification for a portfolio.

(2) Real Estate is a tax favored asset and has great use for sheltering current income by depreciation as well as avoiding capital gain taxes by using 1031 exchanges rather than outright sales. Capital gains taxes can be extended and paid over years by selling on an installment contract.

(3) The population of the U.S. is expanding which is a secular trend. Residential Real Estate is a basic need such as food and is always in demand.

(4) Real Estate has tremendous capital appreciation potential via a leverage investment (standard 30 year fixed rate mortgage) and one that everyone understands.

(5) Value retention with internal, consistent growth due to the principal reduction; a characteristic of a simple, amortized residential mortgage.

(6) The best reason is cash flow. I want cash on cash return, a property projected to increase in value, and an area with a history of rental increases that will provide increasing spendable INCOME!

Real estate is a separate asset class and is traditionally much less volatile than the stock & bond market. There is no daily, or for that matter, moment to moment quote on your holding and by its nature Real Estate is a much more long term investment. Ask a stockbroker what long term is and they may reply 2 weeks to 6 months whereas my long term is 10 years. I have a very long term horizon. I fully expect to go through at least 2 up & down Business Cycles and hold my investments through the cycle. If the stock market crashed and values plummeted most investors would want to sell! Contrarily, I want to hold and receive the Cash Flow that would mitigate the downtrend in the economy. Real Estate is separate from the Stock and Bond Market often benefiting from it's troubles; essentially Real Estate is a basic commodity like food and gasoline. The price of gas may go up and down, but people need gasoline and always buy; like a farmer, I sometimes have bumper crops and sometimes just good crops, but I ALWAYS HAVE A CROP. Further, everyone needs a place to live and there has never been a shortage of tenants! As a seasoned Investor, I have found Time is my greatest friend, the value of my investments will rise, and with it, the revenue from my cash flow will grow significantly. Ten years of rental increases substantially raises my monthly cash flow.

Real Estate often shelters a portion the cash it generates as well as other current income through a depreciation schedule on Federal Income Tax. I buy Real Estate for its cash flowing properties, but I am grateful for the tax shelter. Your involvement in the business of leasing your property and your current income will determine the amount of Depreciation taken on your Federal Tax; one is classified as an Active or Passive Investor. I am in the business of Real Estate and as such I can shelter a greater amount. Check with a tax professional.

Capital gains are a wonderful byproduct of a successful investment; Real Estate allows for an exchange of properties without triggering a capital gain tax liability. The tax liability is carried forward to the next property as long as the transaction is "like for like." This feature has been greatly expanded to include almost anything considered Real Estate and gives enormous flexibility to

12

adjust holdings, update properties, upgrade properties, or even move to another state; all by deferring the tax. Consider a $100K gain in a property I want to sell to buy a larger property. If I paid 20% to Uncle Sam my debt would be $20,000 greater in the new property and my cash flow that much less, but via a 1031 exchange – <u>ALL</u> the proceeds are available and will continue to earn. Consider the difference of a normal stock mutual fund where 20% of the stocks are turned every year resulting in a 20% taxable event; over 5 years a considerable amount has been paid to the IRS rather than adding to the investment returns!

In the 1980's, depreciation schedules were accelerated to the ludicrous allowing investors to make money by saving money on their taxes; the "Investors lose money, but make it up in volume" theory! Thus many investors bought properties solely on the property's Federal Income Tax shelter value, not on it's economic value. Badly located, overpriced properties were sold at monthly losses which became pretty significant over an annual basis, but provided Triple Depreciation and huge Tax Savings. When the Congress changed the tax laws at the same time as the S & L debacle hit in the late '80's, Investors registered huge losses often resulting in Liquidation and Bankruptcy. In those turbulent times, because I had bought good properties for their economic and intrinsic value, I easily rode out the downturn. I was never threatened with a loss and my cash and credit were intact to buy when the bottom was at hand. I buy excellent, cash flowing properties with depreciation as a bonus! Also, even though a 1031 Exchange is tax-deferred, I buy to keep forever and would sell only if the neighborhood was no longer growing and my property was threatened! Here is an example of a property I purchased as the economy turned in 1984. This property has been continually leased and over the years and the tenants have completely paid the mortgage balance. A Principal Reduction plan was instituted 3 years after acquisition; the rental increases were applied to the mortgage principal balance which resulted in a Free and Clear property well ahead of schedule.

Long Term Hold Case Study
XXXX Main Dr., Phoenix, AZ.

This property has been in the rental portfolio since it was acquired in March of 1984. It has been free and clear since 2002 and leased continuously.

Purchased price new 3/21/1984 .... $ 44,600

Down Payment 20% 9,200

Upgrades: very minimal, gravel, mini-blinds 1400

Total Acquisition Cost $46,000

Current Value 4/2015 .... $140,000

Net Annual Cash Flow 6,000

Fully Depreciated ($46,400 @ 85% = 37,900 base)
28% bracket 10,600

Cash Flow Extracted over 30 years 125,000

Total Return $275,600

$9,200 has returned $275,000 over the last 31 years and continues to add Investment Return.

The Real Estate Investment Return: $275,000 / 9200 = 29.891 times the investment

ALMOST 3,000%

This investment still keeps sending monthly cash flow and keeps appreciating!!!

It can be a legacy for generations to come.....multiply this by 10, 20, or 30 properties!!!!!

Strategic Real Estate

All things cycle and the economies of the World are no different. Every year, the Globe becomes more intertwined: events in China, Russia, Greece, or Brazil will affect employment and growth in other Nations. Red Flags are growing and Strategic Real Estate needs to be reviewed for acquisition to be used as a "Lifeboat" during any Fiscal Turmoil. Profits from Stock and Bond portfolios should be considered as a source of funds to purchase quality cash flowing Real Estate Assets. My research leads me to believe that after the next Recession, the Greatest Bull Market in Real Estate will start. Meanwhile, cash flowing properties will easily mitigate any downturn and serve as a spring board to launch into the next recovery.

Real estate is in a secular trend which means there is a great force of population that will over time grow the price of my properties. The demographics are of an expanding population, although aging. The so-called Millennial generation will have children and lead to more teenagers in the year 2030 than ever in our history. Immigration is a continued topic of discussion because the United States is the only real light in the world and continues to attract people from around the Globe. This trend is excellent for housing, a basic need, and should help insure <u>real</u> growth and appreciation without factoring inflation. Simple economics of supply & demand should increase the value; Will Rogers said "Land-they aren't making any more of that". The Federal Government's Bureau of Labor & Statistics can help locate areas to purchase. Southern Calif. is expected to grow from 35 million to 55 million and we in Phoenix, AZ are projected to have job growth, population growth, & personal income growth in all categories. The Phoenix MSA been ranked as one of the Top Two Growth markets in the nation, second only to Houston. Phoenix, AZ population will double to over 7.5 million by 2025. These statistics are a guide and a view to the future of the value of rent and price, but several markets in the US have excellent growth projections.

I want to stress that I buy properties on the merit of their investment value and not on any tax advantage. Tax advantage is a bonus and an enhancement of my investment; I am grateful, but my goal is <u>Financial Freedom</u> via cash flow from my rentals. Further in the Guide we will discuss the purchase of properties, but I buy to keep for a very long time and selling or exchanging is <u>expensive</u>. I am an investor, not a trader!

I buy Real Estate and wait; time is my friend! Appreciation is wonderful and the long term secular trend is up; the term the "Trend is our Friend" is particularly evident for long term Real Estate investing. I am experiencing about a 3% appreciation per year, not spectacular, but certainly sustainable. My appreciation seems to correlate with job growth and population increases which as I have stated is in a secular uptrend. Real Estate is generally purchased with a standard, amortized mortgage of 15-30 year duration with a 20-25% down. This is leverage! Take an example of a $100K purchase with 20% down ($20K) and an 80% ($80K) loan. I experience a 3% appreciation or $3,000 increase in value on a 100K property, but I leveraged this purchase. I have a $3,000 gain on a $20,000 investment. Because I leveraged my investment in a very conservative fashion my gain is not 3% but 15% on my cash portion of the investment. Real estate is not as volatile as the stock or bond markets and there are no margin calls, but real estate investors get the benefit of leverage by the nature of accepted financing practice.

The additional advantage of this investment is it is leveraged with a standard, amortized mortgage. The characteristics of which provide a monthly gain via the principal reduction and over many years this small gain becomes an enormous gain leading to a free and clear property, all without adding any additional capital other than my initial investment.

All these benefits are wonderful, but my primary reason for purchasing residential rental properties is cash flow! I look to purchase properties that will return cash on cash after <u>all expenses</u> have been paid. I look to receive a cash return after Principal & Interest, taxes, insurance, H.O.A., pool service, management fee, and an <u>escrow</u> for future repairs. This is an initial return and over years I will grow my return. As an example of a 3% appreciation rate also affects our rental rates. An initial $1000/mo rental generates approximately $300/mo net cash flow for us. A 3% rental appreciation on $1000 per month rent is $30.00 which increases our cash flow from $300 to $330 or 10% increase on the monthly cash on cash return! Every year my monthly income has increased, with my strategy anyone can do this.

I will outline a strategy to accumulate and keep great wealth that is dependable and understandable. Anyone who has the <u>desire</u> and the <u>will</u> to start will succeed if they follow my plan! I have found that a goal of 10 residential rentals will provide sufficient income for my needs. I do not believe I am unique and for most people 10 rentals should pay their current costs. This is by no means an absolute and depending on <u>your</u> needs and <u>your</u> lifestyle and your starting point will determine <u>how much is enough</u>! The long term goal is to achieve not only the cash flow but to eventually have the properties free and clear and protected in a trust.

My goal is to actualize & empower my life as well as the lives of future generations. I will teach my children my strategy so they will be empowered. I believe in the saying "if you do not want your children to go hungry, teach them to fish."

The Strategy: A House a Year

Here is my strategy: Save your money, cut your costs, save your money, earn more, save your money, and purchase 10 residential properties in 10 years from now.

My strategy is to accumulate assets that give value, stability, and still grow while producing a high yield of cash flow. My favorite asset is residential rental real estate.

Owning rental real estate has tremendous benefits:

(1) Value retention with growth of equity due to principle balance reduction.

(2) Diversification of assets: does not necessarily parallel the stock & bond markets and does exceptionally well outside of retirement plans.

(3) Special tax treatment: special Depreciation and Exchange privileges to defer capital gains indefinitely as well as installment sales treatment. No social security tax on earned rental income.

(4) Leverage investment: tremendous accentuated appreciation potential of both value and cash on cash returns.

(5) Secular demographic trend of increasing population which over time will increase prices.

(6) Personal control and familiarity

(7) High cash on cash return; monthly distribution.

The first benefit of value retention I will elaborate on in my strategy for purchasing, but the obvious and easiest source of growth is simply someone else is making the mortgage payment! Due to the nature of a typical mortgage, the balance is reduced each month. Like Magic, the principal portion included in the monthly payment, will reduce the financed balance to zero and substantial wealth is created for our benefit, but paid by someone else!

If I bought a rental property every year for 10 years priced at $150,000, invested $30,000 as down payment, and used a 30 year amortized loan, which is easily obtained, after 30 years I would have a property become Free and Clear every year for the next 10 years. Enormous wealth and cash flow would have been created thanks to my tenants. My great friend, Time, will create wealth for me easily, on schedule, and dependably. I decide how much wealth I want and it will come. Consider purchasing 10 homes between the age of 30 & 40. Anyone who has had children will realize how quickly time passes; by the time the Investor is 60 look what has happened: ten homes at $150K = $1.5 million dollars. A typical Rental purchased for $150,000 and leases for $1000/ month has $150 per month in taxes and insurance, $100/mo management & sinking fund, $610 Principal & Interest. (I am being very conservative). Over 30 years $300K has been invested and if there is no appreciation, no growth, no cash flow, no tax advantage; the $300K will grow to $1,500,000. Every year for 10 years, one of the properties mortgage obligation will be eliminated and $610 income per month can be added to the Cash Flow until all 10 are Free & Clear. Time will give $6100 additional income plus whatever the original cash flow of $140/mn grows to over 30 years. I should easily project $7500 to $10,000 per month.

The Strategy does not stop at 10 homes; continue to add at least one property per year. Think what wealth and income would accumulate over 40 years of investing. I also do not amortize over 30 years, but I accelerate the principal reduction by adding a portion of the rental increases every year to the payment in the form of principal reduction. By adding one payment extra per year on a 30 year amortized loan it will pay off in 18+ years, saving thousands of dollars in interest! Many variations exist, but the strategy is the same: reduce the debt as quickly as possible to establish free & clear properties.

Principal Reduction Strategy

O ne of my favorite Principal Reduction Strategies is to retain the first 3 years of rent increases to build reserves and accumulate cash for more properties. Years 4 through 7, I add the rent increase to the payment and begin reducing the debt; four years of adding 3% to the payment will reduce the loan from 30 years to less than 18 years saving tens of thousands of dollars.

Free and clear properties lose the benefit of leverage which we will explore in greater detail, but a Free & Clear property mitigates risk. A Free & Clear property will always generate cash flow in good markets or bad markets, Free& Clear Income Properties allow for greater flexibility of rental income, and possible future installment sale, but also the cash flow is greatly enhanced.

Diversification

The second benefit is diversification. I believe strongly in personal retirement plans. However most qualified plans are invested in securities of the stock & bond markets; they could be ETFs of commodities, but expressed in shares. Further, these plans are intended for the later, retirement years and not for current use. My Strategy allows the Investor to enjoy the Investment throughout his Lifetime, rather than waiting until retirement. IRA's and Keogh's typically use securities that have a 10 year return of 7.4%, but along the way there has been great volatility, tremendous swings up & down causing many sleepless nights and currently, many believe the valuations are overdone and unsustainable, even risky. Further, valuations are on a moment by moment basis, totally out of control of the average investor. Although the ability to liquidate instantly is certainly an advantage in many circumstances, there is a temptation to try to time the market; long term investment sometimes gets sold in a panic whereas the very nature of Real Estate is geared toward long term investing forcing an investor to stay with their plan or strategy.Currently,Volatility and Risk appear to be rising in the Equity markets.

Some research indicates that although the average returns have been averaging 7+%, many investors have remained in cash and are not fully invested nor invested while the markets were cheap and undervalued. These investors are reported to receive less than 3% return preferring to remain conservative and remain on the sidelines. These investors have been decimated by the low interest rates of CD's, Money markets, and conservative Bond Funds. A conservative investment in Income Real Estate may be a strategy to preserve

Capital and earn a return to help supplement Social Security and any Pensions.

Real Estate is a separate asset class and performs on its own parameters – not the financial market's. Although Real Estate is influenced by economic conditions, as in any business, Real Estate or housing (shelter) is a basic need like food & water and is much more stable being affected by population, job growth, infrastructure (like freeways & shopping centers) and demographics much more than the daily changes in the interest rates quoted by Wall Street. I believe my retirement plans should hold the securities such as stocks and bonds, but our personal assets should be in Real Estate, which has the added benefit of favorable tax treatment. However currently, in my estimation, the risk associated with the Equities Markets warrants a reduced exposure; yet the potential in the Real Estate Market is so compelling, that Real Estate Income Properties should be included in a large portion of any pension, IRA, or Keogh.

Depreciation

This brings us to the third reason which is depreciation of the building structure and tax-deferred exchanges. Part of the overbuilding of the 80's was a direct result of extremely liberal depreciation allowances accorded Real Estate investments. Real Estate investors could lose money on their investments, however they could shelter enough income from tax obligations to be profitable. Therefore, properties were bought on the tax benefits not the economic benefits of the Real Estate Investment. Tax burdened investors paid too much for properties but received their compensation via tax relief. This caused properties to be built without regard to market research, freeway and road access, improper amenities, etc. They were built and bought without the goal of being successfully occupied & utilized. Congress changed the rules in 1985.

The tax code change put sanity back into depreciation and placed personal income and involvement requirements on investors. Depreciation deductions are still valid and still shelters ordinary income from taxation for most investors and is wonderful, but check with your tax preparer for actual benefits. For most people, lots of ordinary income will be sheltered and not taxed which is a huge benefit! For example, an investor earning $40,000 of taxable income with an $80K rental can reduce the taxable amount by depreciating the building, not the land. An $80,000 purchase may be considered $15,000 land value and $65,000 of structure value which can be depreciated over 27.5 years or $2363 per year reducing the $40,000 taxable income to $37,637, a savings of $661 ($2363 @.28 tax rate). I buy my rental properties because they are good properties with good long term growth prospects and cash flow returns within my parameters, but thank you "Uncle Sam" for any extra.

Tax Deferred 1031 Exchange

The most outstanding tax benefit feature of residential rentals is the ability to sell one property and buy another without triggering a tax liability by trading properties using a 1031 exchange. Over the course of holding properties, my properties appreciate or gain in value; I take my depreciation and shelter current income which lowers the basis in my properties. Should I sell them, I would be liable to pay taxes on the difference of the depreciated cost and the sales price. For example: simply put, if I held an $80K home for 10 years and depreciated $2363 per year my cost basis is no longer $80K but $56,400 and when I sell this property for $160K for a hefty $80K gain I would owe capital gains on $103,600 ($80,000 + 10 x $2363 = 23,600 rounded). By using a 1031 exchange, I carry forward the gain to the new property and resume the depreciation with a new basis. The tax is deferred, possibly forever. If the estate planning is done properly, the heirs will inherit at the stepped up basis and the start fresh!

The requirements for a 1031 are very simple:

(1) purchase a property for equal or greater in net sales price.

(2) Re-invest all the new equity in the replacement property.

(3) Obtain equal or greater debt on the replacement property.

(4) One must exchange "like kind" property;
like kind properties being very open but Real
Estate to Real Estate is fine.

Investors can accomplish almost any investment strategy by using a deferred exchange including diversification, improved cash flow, greater leverage, relocation, etc. Tax deferred exchanges allow me to carry huge capital gains forward without the loss of earning power on that portion a tax payment would claim. I am earning on Uncle Sam's deferred Tax!

Long Term Loans

T he fourth advantage is leverage. I have approximately 20% of the cost of the investment in my personal capital, the balance I finance through the use of an ordinary amortized mortgage, 80% of the cost of our investment is "OPM" other people's money!. A 4 to 1 Ratio, this is leverage; it allows me to control more properties and increase my returns.

As an example, the houses in my area of Arizona have average a 3 – 5% appreciation per year; not skyrocketing but steady. I could put my money in the money market with no risk and receive less than 1% or take more risk in the Equities market for a little more. I chose Real Estate where I am leveraged 4 to 1! An increase of 3% is a 15% return on my portion. A $100K home has a loan of $80K or 80%, if it appreciates 3% or $3,000 the increase to me is a $3,000 gain on $20,000 investment or $3,000 / $20,000 = 15% return on my capital invested. The same is true of rental increases. For example, if my $1,000/mo rental has a 3% rate increase it is $30/mo X 12 months or $360/yr. If my initial rental cash on cash return was $2400 or $200/mo. A 3% rate increase is $30 or 30/200 = 15% increase in our cash flow – 15% just in rent increases.!

Over 5 years with a very modest increase, I have a sizable cash on cash return which is generating excellent free cash flow which can be used to purchase more rentals and increase my wealth, reduce my loan balance which will increase my wealth, or spent which will increase my well-being and fill my "fun-bank"!

Real Estate has been and continues to be in a secular demographic trend with a predictable and projected increase in value which follows the demographics of the US. Information can be obtained from the government on any local area. Southern California is projected to increase from 35 million people to 55 million people in the next 20 years; metropolitan Phoenix, AZ is predicted to almost double it's population in 10 years!. Housing is a basic commodity subject to the market forces of supply and demand; where job growth goes, so does appreciation <u>and</u> almost at the same rate. Choose carefully, buy, and let the market work.

I also love Real Estate because everyone is familiar with it. I can touch it. I can become very good at values & property condition very quickly. I can assess property potential and I can personally view an area or neighborhood and determine the trend of appreciation and growth. I can do the maintenance myself or hire it out, but the work is not so technical as to confuse me. In short, we all live in houses and we all can understand them.

Cash Flow

My favorite reason to invest in Real Estate is cash flow! All other reasons are an enhancement of our priority goal which is to receive a dependable stream of income! If I cannot receive a return on my cash after all costs, I will wait until I can. I want my cash flow to grow at least 3% per year (in a leverage investment, it will be greater). I recognize that sometimes markets are lean and sometime they are rich, but I always think long term and I want to average over 10 years. I have for the last 20 years exceeded these averages; anyone can!

My strategy is to buy excellent properties that I will keep forever! I am not a trader who buys and sells, I find the costs are very high and much greater wealth is achievable by accumulating appreciating assets that generate meaningful cash flow. My goal is to buy 10 properties in 10 years. I can accumulate more or less, but I find 10 properties will pay the expenses of most middle class Americans. The goal can be modified to adjust to anyone's lifestyle and starting point; if you are young and just entering the work force or are well established and a high income earner, the strategy is the same.

One of the great real estate investors, Harry Helmsley, was interviewed about how he had created such enormous wealth. He had purchased great trophy properties like the Empire State Building and the Helmsley Palace Hotel in New York City and had enjoyed their benefits. When asked how he knew it was time to sell his face went blank, he paused and stated "I don't think I ever sold any of my properties." Wow! Can you imagine buying properties for forty years and never selling any? What enormous wealth, what great intrinsic knowledge he possessed. Harry Helmsley grew older and his net worth grew with him.

Living Well to 100 Years

Today we have an excellent chance of living to 100 years or beyond! The numbers of people in their 80-90's is enormous and growing. Being 100 years old was an oddity just a generation ago, but not anymore. What would a pension and fixed income portfolio of a person who retired in 1960 be worth today? Probably not a pretty picture. Inflation would have eroded the purchasing power to the point a 1960 retiree would be dependent on others. This brings us to the art of living well to 100 years old.

I was told a story about a retiring executive who was asked about his career. He replied "I can remember missing my six year old's piano recital because of an important business deal, but I can't remember the business deal itself!" Such wisdom! A job is a way of making money not a way to fulfill oneself! Enjoy yourself more and spend time with your family because your career will end, but your family never will.

A tremendous benefit of my strategy is it is **not** intended as a retirement plan, but rather as a means to economic freedom. I do not want to lose sight of what is really important in my life and I do not intend to be retired before I can start living, but rather slowly become free to follow my dreams by building very useable wealth. Although I believe in Keogh's, IRA's and pension funds, they are severely limited in accessing this wealth. Holding Real Estate outside of pension funds allows for access to the investment as well the returns on the investment and still receive some tax benefits. The growth factor of existing properties as well as any addition to the portfolio will gradually become meaningful over time and the goal is to have greater investment income than W2 or work related income. The goal is to enjoy the wealth created prior to 59½!

Useable Income Prior to Retirement

Medical advances are straining the Social Security System. When Social Security was first originated, the average life expectancy was in the mid-60's for an average American Male; suggesting only a few years of retirement. Now, Life expectancies are well into the 80's with some studies suggesting late 90's to early 100's for more and more of the population. Further, advances in anti-aging are providing a much more active life style with hip and knee replacements, heart stents, and bio medicines. The challenge not only in the US, but across the world is how to live well into an extended retirement of 30-40 years.

Income requirements will increase not decrease as ones time expands to actualize life. The dilemma is how to not only maintain Wealth and Income, but to grow Wealth. Risk needs to be mitigated as an unfortunate part of growing old, a catastrophic loss or downturn could make recovery difficult. With increased longevity comes increased volatility as individuals live through more business cycles and demographic shifts and much more Geo-political change. As one ages, the investment portfolio should season and become less risky. This is particularly true of rental properties with simple amortized loans paying off on a dependable scale. As free and clear properties grow in the portfolio, **RISK** is greatly reduced. A portfolio needs to address many possible outcomes, but a strategy to continually produce free and clear cash flowing properties is a very liberating Strategy.

My Strategy is to build wealth slowly over a life time and increase the cash flow to exceed all cash requirements. To slowly become free to work or not, to volunteer or not, to pursue dreams, goals, aspirations, because a **Money Machine** has been created to produce useable cash every month; cash to fund "The Bucket List". Growing old then becomes fun when retirement gives you all of the fun you had as a kid, but no cash restrictions to slow the adventure. You can Cruise the Nile, travel to Antarctica, walk the Great Wall of China, buy motorcycles, campers, jets, etc. You will be free! Purchasing properties and re-amortizing them to quickly reduce the balance should continue throughout ones lifetime ensuring loads and loads of dependable monthly income with the added bonus of pension funds and Social Security. Buy a property every year, get your children and grandchildren to start the Strategy and build a Generational Legacy.

The simple amortized real estate loan is scheduled to pay itself off in a predetermined time frame. My goal is financial freedom and to create wealth and cash flow as great as I wish. Therefore, by re-amortizing my mortgage loans I can structure the payoff to any time frame I desire. My strategy is to buy and keep properties for 10 years or forever if the neighborhood is still growing and appreciating and gradually over time payoff the rentals and have at least 10 Free & Clear properties. Once the properties are Free & Clear, I lose the leverage multiplication factor, but I mitigate risk! Without a loan on my properties I can withstand any downturn in the economy or even the worst scenario which would be a protracted deflationary spiral. My investment will be maintained in current real dollars which would maintain my lifestyle in Inflationary or Deflationary scenarios.

During the Real Estate Bubble debacle of 2008-2010, the value of the properties here in Phoenix plunged from exorbitant levels to below replacement costs; a decline in some properties by 60-70%; catastrophic for over-leveraged owners. Those that heeded warnings sold marginal properties and raised cash; the plunge in prices became an enormous buying opportunity. However, the rental revenue never dipped below 15% of peak and continued to return cash on a consistent basis. Times were tough, but the properties were a "Life Boat". Further, the cost of maintenance, insurance premiums, and taxes all declined mitigating the decline in the rent revenue. Currently, in 2015, all rent levels have been restored and an above average rent increase of 8% is projected for the next year not only here in Phoenix, but also above average rent increases for the rest of the US. Real Estate prices have recovered, but not to the values associated with the "Bubble" prior to the Great Recession.

My strategy is to add to the principal reduction a little at a time to payoff early; there is no "downside", after owning my rentals and receiving cash flow for 30 years, my tenants have paid the other 80% of the initial investment. Wait! 30 years is a lifetime! Is it? Demographic research predicts average life expectancies to easily extend until the mid 80's and a record amount of centurions are all going to need cash flow. If you retire at 65 and live to 100 what will your portfolio generate? 100% of your needs; or if there is any inflation over 35 years – maybe only 30% of your needs and you will be poor living on the kindness of others. A Very scary thought!

Most people expect to retire and live on a pension or savings for the rest of their lives. For retirement, most people have their homes Free & Clear, they have purchased most of the furnishings, beds, silverware, linens, etc that they are likely to own, their children are out of school and on their career paths, and upon retirement daily expenses should drop substantially as business lunches, office rent, attire, commuting, equipment are phased out and their income therefore will stretch further, which is true. Additionally, as they age, Medicare health benefits will start and health insurance costs will be reduced. Initially, a retiree's cost of living is lowered, but look what happens to the purchasing power of a $50,000 annual fixed income vs. a rental income of $50K with a very moderate inflation rate of 2%:

Fixed Income Portfolio	Income Properties Portfolio
Year 1 $50,000	(1) $50,000
Year 2 $49,000	(2) $51,000
Year 3 $48,020	(3) $52,020
Year 4 $47,059	(4) $53,060
Year 5 $46,118	(5) $54,121

The effects of inflation become very evident as well as the benefits to a Real Estate portfolio creating in only 5 years a 20% difference in purchasing power as fixed income loses purchasing power and the Real Estate portfolio increases due to rental rate increases. The rate of 2% is extremely mild, 4% is still mild but wildly bullish for Real Estate.

Year:		Year;	
(0) $50,000		(0) $50,000	
(1) $48,000		(1) $52,000	
(2) $46,080		(2) $54,080	
(3) $44,237		(3) $56,243	
(4) $42,467		(4) $58,493	
(5) $40,768		(5) $60,832	

This is just the income stream for real estate not factoring in the other benefits such as constant principal reduction, tax advantages, and appreciation. Further, my favorite ally, TIME, will further boost the income stream when the loan pays off by the absence of a mortgage payment. Here is an example of a typical investment rental's appreciation over a 10 year period at a conservative 4% annual rate: my 1980's rental purchase: $60,000 @ 4% **appreciation** = (0) 60K;

Year	(1) $62,400	(6) $75,920
	(2) $64,890	(7) $78.950
	(3) $67,490	(8) $82.110
	(4) $70,190	(9) $85,360
	(5) $72,990	(10) $88,800

A $28,800 increase in value plus the **rental** value has grown as follows:

$650 initial rent:

Year	(1) $676	(6) $822
	(2) $703	(7) $855
	(3) $731	(8) $889
	(4) $760	(9) $925
	(5) $790	(10) $962

A $312/mo increase in cash flow on a typical rental such as a 1983 Purchase of $60,000 @ 80% = 48K @ 8%: $650/mn Rent

48K @ 8% =	$352.32
Tax $	50.00
Ins. $	25.00
Mngt. $	50.00
Repairs	$50.00

Monthly total expenses: $527.00

The initial monthly cash flow in year one is $650-527 = $123 initial net cash flow to a $435/month cash flow in year 10, over a 350% increase in cash flow. Annualized the cash flow grows from $1476 to $5,220. Appreciation has added $12,000 increase in equity not factoring in principal reduction. Why sell such a great investment! I suggest you keep the properties forever with the goal of all free & clear properties allowing for growth and a very attractive cash flow.

Let me use an example of a property I bought in Phoenix, AZ in 1983. I purchased (XXXX Main, Phoenix, AZ) for $44,900 using a 13.5% mortgage & refinancing in 1987 at 9%. I held the property through real estate downturns in Arizona and by 1998, my payment was $380 and my rental income was $780, a $400 delta. Adding in management & a sinking fund for $100, my net cash flow is $300/month. The annual free cash flow was $3600, my cash invested is $9500. The Return On Investment becomes $3600/$9500 = **37.9%** cash on cash return. The property also has a $67/month principal reduction for $804 a year which is $3600 + $804 or $4404 a <u>year</u> on a $9500 investment for a **46.3%** return. But wait it is now worth $80K for an appreciation of $35,100 over 15 years or $2,340 a year (about 5%) or $4404 + 2340 = $6744 on a $9500 investment or **70.9%** per year return! But wait, we also depreciated the property resulting in tax savings! <u>Is this great or what!!</u>

The cost of the Property remains fixed, the initial Capital invested remains constant. The property not only generates consistent cash flow, but generates cash for future repairs. No additional Capital should ever be needed! The rent continues to grow and add to free cash flow. The Mortgage continues to decline scheduled to payoff courtesy of my tenants. The purchase of all of my properties was thoughtful and purposeful; bought in the pathway of growth with expectations of consistent appreciation. Therefore, I can expect these rates of returns to continue. I am not unique and this Strategy can be used fully anywhere.

Another example of a recent purchase in North Phoenix:

This was purchased 1/2015 for a small Retirement Plan. These are actual numbers and returns. Most qualified plans are restricted to cash investing and do not receive the benefit of leverage. The property was leased by tenants driving by just after closing and while the standard clean up afforded to all portfolio properties was underway.The tenants were very willing to wait a few days while the property was readied. The property was purchased for cash and will consistently return a monthly income which is projected to increase next year. The initial cash -on-cash return is slightly above 6%.

XXXX Main Dr, Phoenix, AZ.

Purchase Price including closing costs; $161,914
Estimated Clean up cost(paint, cleaning, landscape, etc) $2,500
Total Acquisition $164,414

Leased per month $1125
Cleaning fee $300
Security Deposit $1125

Expenses:
Taxes: $874/12 = ...$74.00
Landlord Policy $455/12 38.00
Monthly HOA 30.00
Vacancy 5% 55.00
Repair Escrow 100.00
Total monthly expenses $295.00

$1125.00 rent - $295.00 monthly expenses = $830 monthly cash flow EVERY MONTH

$830 X 12 = $9,960 first year cash flow/ $164,414 = **6.05%** cash on cash return

This was sold to a very conservative Pension Fund. By leveraging with a standard home loan, the return can be greatly enhanced.

If this had been leveraged conservatively with 30% down, $48,500 an additional charge of $1680 would probably apply plus the clean up costs for a total of $166,094 Acquisition Cost and a total cash invested of $52,600.

Mortgage payment: $112,000 at 4.5% = $567 +295 = $862 monthly payment

Should a leveraged purchased been used to acquire the property:

Financed monthly cash flow: $1125 – 862 = $263.00 Annualized: $3156.00

Total cash in transaction: $52,680

Cash on Cash return: $3156 / 52,680 = **5.9%**

Principal reduction first year: $1803 + 3156 = $4959 / 52,600 = **9.4%**

1st year depreciation:$160,500 less lot value of 15% = $136,000 over 27.5 years = $4945

Deductible loss (depreciation) of $4945 in a 28% bracket = $1384

Add in Depreciation: $1384 + 3156 + 1803 = $6343 / 52,600 = **12.04%**

Over twice the ROI can be achieved without factoring in the inevitable appreciation from the upgrades.

The Purchase Price was $161,900 including closing costs. Within 30 days of this sale, another property in the same neighborhood, built by the same builder, with the same floor plan, only 2 blocks away appraised for $7,500 more than the acquisition price; a vindication for good shopping and excellent negotiations; verifying the property was purchased below value. As a cash transaction, the additional ROI would be an additional 4% ($7500 / 161,900 = 4.6%) on top of the 6% would give an initial return of 10%. As the property appreciates, value would be added. A typical year of 3% would add over $5000 per year driving the first year ROI to 13%.

On a Financed transaction the returns are greater: $7500 additional bonus on $52,600 is a whopping 14.25% and an additional 3% first year appreciation would add $5,000 on $52,600 or a potential 9.5% boost if the property appreciated jut 3% for an incredible 12.04% + 14.25% + 9.5% = 35.79%.

As you can see, after a few years, this becomes very serious money. Compound this by a new property every year and the Portfolio is growing exponentially!

A leveraged property has additional characteristics that afford greater returns. The purchase was at the very bottom of the selling range as a duplicate model appraised for $168,000 within 30 days of the closing; a $7500 valuation add on without any extensive remodeling or rehabilitating! The overriding reason to purchase properties is for the Income Stream they provide. As part of the strategy, I try to buy at the bottom of the sales range, as all properties age differently and are all unique, but similar particularly so in production subdivisions. The sales range can be quite wide depending on upgrades and condition, however, a forced appreciation can be achieved by returning the building to area standards or above. Often, much greater value add situations are available by purchasing distressed properties and rehabilitating them. Huge increases in both value and rent are achieved. Had this property been leveraged as in my financed illustration; purchasing below market and upgrading to my rental standards, the adjusted ROI would have been $7500 / $52,600 (30% down) = 14.25% additional. The actual ROI would be 12.3% + 14.25% = a whopping 26.55% first year return, excluding any appreciation.!!

As one retires, or as I suggest, partially retire, one has time that needs to be filled. I travel extensively with my children and that is what drives my train! Travel is not cheap! I need income to actualize my life and retirees will realize the same. The sad reality is most people do not expect to live as long as they do and outlive their resources. It is not unusual to live to 85 thus 20 years past productive and high income age. There will be more and more people living into their 90's and 100's than ever experienced in history. Contrary to popular beliefs, expenses incurred during one's business life do not disappear, but only take a different form.

I will always require my investments to grow and to produce income to pay for my daily life. I never want to stop buying properties. If at the age of 40 a property is bought every year until the age of 70, a different property would payoff every year until the age of 100 boosting income, wealth, & purchasing power by the strategy of the simple 30 year amortized loan. As I age, I will travel and have fun until I cannot go anymore, when I stop, my wealth will not! **If I continue to purchase and use a simple amortized fixed rate loan as financing, I can continually INCREASE my Income and Wealth as I age. I will never outlive my MONEY!**

Unfortunately, many of my friends and acquaintances are high income earners and are insulated by their wages. Very few plan for a pro-longed illness or a disability. Retirement is a long way off. They live well, but God help them if they are laid off or downsized or sick; the income stops. If they want to take the summer off and travel to Europe, China, the Far East, or stay in a beach condo in Maui (as I am now), the income stops and because they cannot withstand 4 months of no income or lost income, they will not go have fun, but instead continue to work! Even though they would rather snorkel than write a legal brief for divorce proceedings, the fact remains that bills come due and cash is needed to pay the costs.

This is the essence of my strategy: to develop a plan to provide income forever. I choose how much Income is Enough, the plan will provide whatever is required. I have chosen a subjective goal of 10 properties in 10 years. Because 10 properties over 10 years will generate the equivalent of an average middle income wage and return approx $50-70,000/yr. The amount of properties required is dependent on one's lifestyle and debt load. I am debt free and strongly advise against all debt except investment debt. Follow my strategy and live your life!

Strategy Plan for Accumulation
– How to Select A Portfolio

I live in Phoenix, Arizona the 6th largest metropolitan area in the United States. Phoenix is expected to double its population in twenty years. The city is dynamic and roads, freeways, schools, shopping centers, hotels, sports complexes and arenas, business centers, etc are being built. This construction changes the demographic make up of the metropolitan area and the paths of growth and expansion. Developers work with the city planners to build neighborhoods to accommodate the increase in population. Land & home prices vary according to the local amenity package as well as access to transportation, the quality of schools, and the distance to work. Freeway development opens up outlying areas but also changes traffic patterns and sometimes results in closing of access to older, established areas creating change. What is true today may not be true tomorrow; for better or worse, metropolitan areas are in a state of flux. A metropolitan area that is dynamic may bring uncertainty, but it also brings tremendous opportunity.

As cities grow, there is a change in the desirability due to this dynamism. I try to anticipate the growth and the change in value brought about by the demographic shifts. I attempt to forecast 10 years into the future as to the areas, values and appreciation rates. I buy affordable homes in the outlying area that <u>will</u> have a strong future amenity package. I buy good properties and wait for future development. The art is recognizing the growth paths the city will take. As an example, freeway development has always brought accelerated appreciation to Real Estate value because it is time of travel not distance that is important. I am aware that everyone wants good freeway access; however, no one wants to be too close to the road! As freeways are built and outlying areas are developed, inner areas start to lose their attractiveness. Growth and appreciation shift to new properties with no economic obsolescence and same or less time of commute. The inner properties will have diminished growth or a regression to the mean of value. These shifts take time but these shifts definitely take place and we as investors need to be aware and re-evaluate our portfolio periodically. Phases of growth for most cities and neighborhoods have been defined as Growth, Maturity, Decline, and Revitalization.

I have earned enormous capital & rental returns by identifying trends early and purchasing before the values have risen outside of my purchasing parameters. (I will discuss the formula a little later.) Every city has an area that is considered the "high rent district". This area is usually disproportionately higher than other sections of the city; indeed, often large production or track builders offer the same model elsewhere with a variance in price of 30% or higher. I try to purchase in the area of highest desirability and still maintain my investment parameter. In other words, I try to purchase the best area I can afford and still maintain my returns. Better areas appreciate faster and hold their value better during economic downturns.

For example, in metropolitan Phoenix, AZ the City of Scottsdale is considered the premier city. Further, the north side of Scottsdale is the most desirable. In the early 1990's when we had a severe recession, developers started McDowell Mountain Ranch. The development had everything. The City of Scottsdale blessed the project because the city's research indicated a huge and imminent influx of population. This development was in the middle of the growth path. Scottsdale Air-Park with 50,000+ jobs was 4 miles away, the new expressway was 2 miles away, the development was on the boundary of the Scottsdale Mountain Preserve and the stunningly beautiful McDowell Mountains. The developers worked with the city and built parks, hiking & biking trails, pools and recreation areas, and the city built a state of the art elementary and middle school along with a library, lighted ball fields, and allowed for a new golf course all before a 10th of the population had arrived. A diamond in the rough!

I purchased at entry level in 1997 for $138,000 and in April of 2000, the homes were re-selling for $192,000. I put 20% down plus costs for $31,000. Less than 3 years later, I had appreciation capital of $54,000 for 174% increase on my cash investment plus the property was purchased within guidelines and I have enjoyed a consistent cash on cash return. Currently in 2015, these properties have grown to almost $350,000 and continue to cash flow. I have experienced a huge return because I was aware of the investment potential in the universe of homes and I knew what I was looking for. Here is my guidelines to find a universe of homes within which to choose prime Real Estate rentals.

Universe of Homes

W hile I am saving my down payment and I have pre-qualified for a loan, I am looking for an excellent piece of property. I want to buy a quality property and keep it forever; therefore I want to be sure when I buy. I need to buy only one per year so that gives me a lot of time to investigate potential rentals.

I have found that first I identify the sections of the metropolitan area with the greatest investment potential. The city or county planning office will have statistics and hopefully a master plan of how the city will develop. By being a good listener and observer, I can easily discern the major paths of growth. As in my example of McDowell Mountain Ranch, all the infrastructure and amenities do not have to be in place, but planned with a foreseeable timetable. This should be a rather large geographic area, but small enough that I can become extremely familiar with the different neighborhoods. Also, my investment universe should not be more than 30 to 40 minutes from my home or office as I will be meeting probable tenants and/or service people.

I have over 20,000 homes within my area and over 300 subdivisions but I have only a handful which will meet our criteria. So even a new home built at a very good price may not be within my parameters and hence not work for my Strategy. Here is my Strategy:

> 1) I buy excellent, well located properties that
>   will appreciate.

2) I intend to keep them forever or until they are no longer appreciating at the same pace as comparable properties.

3). I buy 3 or 4 bedroom homes with 2 or more baths, and covered parking for at least 2 cars.

4) I buy single family residential homes with backyards in areas where it is predominantly owner-occupied.

5) I buy homes where the amenity package is excellent.

6). I need cash flow.

I do not buy:

1). Properties on or backing commercial streets, shopping areas, or have any locational problems such as airport or road noise, industrial parks, etc that will impact desirability.

2) I generally do not buy condos or townhouses as the Homeowner Association fees are out of my control and will certainly increase.

3). I generally do not buy 1 or 2 bedroom homes.

I do buy:

1) Fix ups

2) REO's, Short Sales, distressed sales with quick closes (remember I am pre-approved and I can act like cash buyers!)

3). Properties priced "on-sale" within our universe of homes or "grand openings" by builders.

My target market and my "niche" is families w/children who will stay and raise their family in my rental, further, I find they do not like the transiency of apartment complexes or the problem elements associated with other tenants. This group will often remain for 5 to 10 years.

I provide clean, well cared for rentals in desirable areas with excellent amenities and a close proximity to transportation. My major competition is the large, well run apartment complexes. I price my rentals to compare with them plus a 5% premium. My philosophy is clean, trim, and paint for a safe environment that will be conducive for long term residency.

My criteria does not seem to be so rigid or exclusive as to exclude many properties, but my final requirement is the <u>most important</u> – an initial free cash flow. I buy homes to rent, not rent homes that I have bought. I am limited as to the price I can pay by the amount of rent I can receive. This cash flow requirement limits the number of communities in my universe and I thus search a smaller area for my purchases.

Negotiating with Knowledge

I live & invest in N. E. Metropolitan Phoenix, AZ which includes North & Northeast Phoenix, and North Scottsdale, AZ. I have identified 15 neighborhoods out of hundreds which are suitable for our investment strategy. I follow the market in these fifteen communities closely as to what is currently for sale and what has recently sold, what nearby upscale apartment complexes are pricing their rentals, as well as how fully occupied they might be. I am aware of what other homes are renting for, if any. As a rule of thumb, in today's current interest rate and tax rate, we need $1100/mo for a $160,000 rental. As the market appreciates so does the rental value and although the prices go up the rent follows to accommodate the price increase. However the two values are not always in sync and by waiting & observing, I find "The Market Always Provides"! I am a patient, long term investor who has learned the values of our selected universe of homes, I have saved my down payment, I am approved for a loan, and I am ready to buy.

A personal acquisition will illustrate how patience and knowledge of values is rewarded. In 1994, I purchased a 3 bedroom home with a small family room, a 2 car carport, and an in ground pool from a C-21 agent representing a pre-foreclosure. I negotiated only on price as I will do any repairs and I only require a short term opportunity to inspect the property. My loan is assured. I paid $65,500. A steal! I currently rent that property for $1060/month and I include chemical service for the pool. Five years later in May of 1999, I purchased a duplicate floor plan in the same neighborhood, but in addition to the pool, it had a fireplace and a 2 car garage. I paid $96,000: A steal! I paid almost $30,000 more, but the property is still undervalued and will cash flow as follows:

$96,000 X 80% loan = $76,900 @ 7.5% - 5 yr arm
$19,200 down   P & I = $537.00
$ 1,500 closing costs   Taxes: $814/12 = $ 67.00
$3,000 est. repairs   Insure. $450/12 $ 38.00
                                          Repair Escrow = $100.00
                                          pool svc = $ 65.00
                        Cost = $807/month
                Rental value = $1075/month

Cash flow = $268/month X 12 = $3,216

Cash on cash = $3,216 = 13.56%
                          23,700

I was patient and when the opportunity arose, I purchased. The property was represented by Coldwell Banker Realty, a fine company, and the seller was relocating. A relocation company was involved. The property was a mess but I could easily repair and clean the house; $1600 of my estimated $3000 was for a pool fence which is not required but I sleep better at night because of it.

I made an offer and the seller countered at $96,000; 4% below their appraisal. There were other buyers and I was competing for the property, but I was an extremely strong, fully approved buyer who was negotiating only on price. All I required was to fully inspect the property no later than 10 calendar days from acceptance. I would do all the repairs. The seller knew I would close as agreed and their concern was alleviated. They could relocate on schedule. I might have shaved a little more off the price, but I have learned long ago not to be greedy. The seller offered me a gift and I gracefully accepted.

I was an excellent buyer and I knew a value. I have a 3% rule: This property had an appraisal of $100,000 "as is". I knew it would be worth $110,000 repaired and cleaned. As an investment, it was attractively priced and certainly "on sale". I would have purchased the property for $100,000 because I could have spent less than $3000 to raise the value to $110,000. I want to spend 97% or less of value therefore 97% of $110,000 is $106,700 for a total acquisition price. $106,700 becomes the top of my acquisition parameter and my "walk away" price would have been $102,000 – (102,000 + 3,000 repairs + 1500 closing costs) at their asking price of $99,900 it was a bargain!

I received an equity position via their $100,000 appraisal (and my verification via my knowledge of my Universe of Homes) of $4,000 the day we closed. I had a total of $23,700 cash contribution:

$19,200 Down payment
1,500 Closing costs
3,000 Repairs
$ 4,000 = 16.8% Immediate return of equity
$23,700

Further, the property was appraised "as is" so the repair cost of $3,000 should be removed to read $4,000/$20,700 = $19.3% return on equity. I could not leave the property in its initial condition and I improved it with paint, cleaning, trimming, and a pool fence which brought the property back up to the higher standards of the neighborhood and the value of $110,000. I had a gain of $14,000 ($96 - $110 = $14,000) prior to renting or $14,000/$23,700 = 59% initial gain on equity!

I have a goal of one property a year, I am patient and I know a good value. I cannot buy a great property at a great price everyday, or every week, nor every time, but I always buy at 97% or less (an easy target to achieve) which always results in a 13% gain immediately and strongly impacts my rental return as well. My goal is to buy good properties and keep them forever. When a good property becomes available, here is my procedure.

I view the property and try to make as detailed an inspection as possible (a **detailed inspection booklet is available**), I verify the value by recent sales and /or appraisals (a **detailed comparison form is also available**), and I rely heavily on my personal judgment based on my personal knowledge of the home in my Universe of Homes. I try to assess the needs and concerns of the seller and I make a written offer.

My example of one of my personal purchases was of a home listed for sale at $99,900 in an area of homes that sell between $100 - $110, this property was at the bottom of the range and was definitely "on sale". Because I want to buy only excellent properties that are attractively priced, I often find myself competing to purchase. Part of the art of negotiations is the solving of problems for the seller. I ask questions such as (1) where are they moving? Is the seller building and perhaps they need to sell and lease back? (2) Is the closing date important? Is there a timing issue – sooner, later, or specific date in mind? If sooner, is there a financial stress such as divorce, foreclosure, etc? (4) Are there issues discovered or known about repairs? Government loans are more difficult to obtain if there are repair issues and generally in the case of fix-ups the seller is unable or unwilling to do the repairs. As a rule I base my offer only on price and try to address the seller's concerns. Remember, price and value are paramount to me, but sometimes price, although important, is not always **THE** overriding issues for sellers! We will go back to our $99,900 purchase example.

There was another offer in addition to mine but my offer addressed the seller's concerns and alleviated them by assuming the responsibility for curing the problem. My purchase offer for the property was to a relocation company hired to handle the transfer of key corporate personnel to another part of the country. The relocation company, in addition to needing to sell the home had 2 problems: (1) timing the sale of the home to coincide with school schedules and leave enough time for their personnel to shop and acquire a new residence, and (2) handle the repairs long distance!

I made an offer with a definite closing date 5 days **after** the transferee was scheduled to move. The Relocation Company's client was allowed to keep their children in school until the end of the school year and I extended the closing with a fully approved loan in place to allow for trips to the new location to purchase a replacement home. I am also very strong financially and I assumed the responsibility to manage the repairs. To the relocation company, it was ideal! Their client had the required time and a flexible, but certain, closing date and the issue of repair & maintenance was alleviated. As investors, it cost me nothing to accommodate the closing date, I had no lease that was due or pressure to move on a certain day and as for repairs, I have found I do a better job for less!

I made my agreement work for the seller and accommodated at every possible issue. I was approved, ready and able to close, and flexible; all I asked was a discount in price. To the seller, I was the preferred buyer. I could close when they wanted and they did not have to clean or paint; to the sellers this was a great value. I was able to win the bidding war and to purchase at a discount even though there was another full price offer! Price was not their greatest concern!

I typically purchase at the bottom of the range in price and do the necessary updating, painting, cleaning, trimming etc to force the value higher. This allows me to re-value the property and maximize the rental rate. I assume I will clean and paint as a cost of doing business and automatically factor it into my cost structure, but more importantly the rental value is enhanced and thus my cash flow.

To restate my Strategy:

(1) I determine my universe of homes from which I will purchase.

(2) I immerse myself in my universe and become extremely knowledgeable of prices, rents, amenities, growth factors, etc.

(3) I make written offers on properties at the bottom of the range with an initial offer 6 to 7% below value addressing the seller's problems (problems become solutions).

(4) I purchase for no more than 97% of low-end value and "walk away" at higher figures.

(5) I want to purchase at least one property a year and keep forever.

(6) I determine the number of rentals by the income I desire.

(7) I raise the rent annually by the rate of growth.

(8) When appropriate, I accelerate the principal reduction with a goal of all free and clear properties.

Free and Clear Strategy

My wealth strategy is a long term strategy with a very subjective 10 property goal. I plan on living well into old age and my goal is to never stop acquiring at least one property per year. Every year my cash flow will increase by the rental rate appreciation and new acquisition. Further, I plan on holding my properties a very long time and thus the fluctuation in market values are reduced and the long term (10 – 30 yrs) of upside appreciation will prevail. My values will achieve tremendous gains. I also mitigate risk by accelerating my principal reduction (paying off the mortgage) whenever I have surplus cash flow.

For example, as my properties age, I enhance them with new paint colors and flooring. I also have aging mortgages that I enhance by adding additional principal to the mortgage payment to payoff early. Anyone can use a simple amortization schedule to find the desired amount necessary to pay the loan off early. As I have learned over time, I have favorite properties that I know I will keep forever. There are many reduction plans available or simple computer programs for the acceleration, but by making one extra payment per year I will save years of interest. By adding 4%, 7% or 10% additional to the principal, tens of thousands of my money can be saved!

Consider a property in its fifth year as a rental with a conservative 3% annual rental increase. Year (1) 800, (2) 824, (3) 848, (4) 873, and (5) 899, I have increased my cash flow by $100 over the initial rent. If I add $50.00 to the payment which typically would be $80K @ 8% = $64K @ 8% or $470 P & I per month, the payment would increase to $520.00 and should that be the only increase I make, the loan would payoff 6 years early and save over $22,000 in interest. Further, I would increase the monthly rent by 3% the sixth year for a $27/month per month cash flow and I would have recovered over 50% of the cash flow designated for principal reduction and all of it the following year. My <u>principal reduction</u> strategy is on its way! Multiply the $22,000 in savings by 10 properties and that is <u>**SERIOUS**</u> money! By accelerating again, any

combination is possible and easily within 20 years, half of the properties could be free and clear.

Five free & clear properties would easily generate $3-4,000/month of dependable, spendable, inheritable, <u>pure cash flow!</u> If I continue to work my Brokerage Practice and did not spend the cash flow, I could roll $35-$45,000/year into paying off other mortgages and by 25 years, I would easily have achieved $1-2 million of free & clear rental properties generating $6-10,000 per month of enjoyable cash! I won't stop at 10 – the amount is limitless!

Finally here is the secret I have learned: <u>THERE IS NO SECRET!</u> ANYONE CAN DO THIS! THERE IS NO LIMIT!

Getting Started

To get started: How to buy, where to buy, what to buy.

(1) Obtain capital – The first Investment Property is the most difficult. It requires one to save money, cut personal and business costs, increase income via 2nd job or increasing business Income. A two income household (team effort) has distinct advantages of extra income and a partner to keep one MOTIVATED.

(2) Qualify & obtain approval for first rental or 1st home to be converted into rental – options VA/FHA, Fannie Mae, Freddie Mac, or private portfolio.

(3) Research Universe of Homes.

(4) Select a property "on sale". Have patience, the market will always provide.

(5) Negotiate with a plan: 3% rule, know as-is value and repaired value.

(6) Paint, replace, trim, standardize.

Strategies:

Zero Coupon Rental or as the Aussies' Say
"Negative Gearing Mate"!!!

There are circumstances when an extremely good property becomes available at a very compelling price. However, the monthly rent is insufficient to pay the monthly cost. High rent areas like California, Washington D.C., New York City, London, Sydney, Tokyo, Hong Kong, etc. are almost all such areas. Cash flow is difficult to obtain and the strategy is to capture enough initial Capital Gain to cushion any negative event should market forces abruptly turn. This is usually a distressed situation and an Investment of Opportunity. Another situation revolves around timing a recovering market or a steadily improving market that factors indicate several years of strong growth; again this is generally a special situation with a pre-determined plan of action. In recent years, there have been several recovering markets across the Globe that have high entry levels, but Demographics and Economics have consistently pushed purchase prices higher. Please refer to the Stages and Phases of Bubbles by **Jean-Paul Rodrigue** as the Mania phase rewards the Investor the most, but this is Real Estate and liquidation can be agonizingly slow at times requiring delicate timing; sometimes it is best to leave the party early! Knowing the phases allows an Investor to gauge whether Risk is Rising.

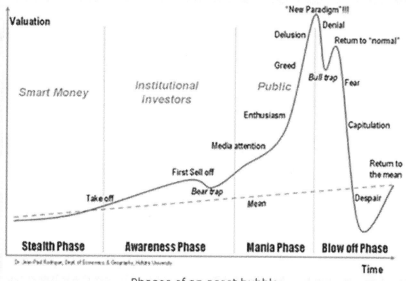

Phases of an asset bubble

A strategy of subsidizing can be used by high wage earners with the goal of growing the revenue over a number of years until the rent finally meets costs. The cost of maintaining the property not covered by the rent becomes an immediate deduction on Income Taxes; one loses money, but re-coups the loss through taxes. This is similar to the accelerated depreciation of the 1980's: lose money, but make it up with deductions!! The strategy is valid only for high wage earners and properties that should be at least cash neutral within 5 years. The value of the property should be extremely compelling as this is a much riskier undertaking.

An example would be a property valued at $800,000 that could be purchased for considerably less, say $650-700,000. The monthly payment could easily exceed $2700 per month plus HOA, Management and a repair escrow for a true break even of closer to $3000+ per month. If the rental market bears that much or more, then a terrific property is available. If the rent covers only $2500 then it must be subsidized, most investors do not like subsidizing properties believing the property should pay them, not they pay the property. High wage earners would be able to recoup part of the loss through Income Tax relief. However, this property is an exceptional piece and at a compelling price! A typical 3% increase in the rent per year on $2500 is $75 per year. Within 6 years, cash flow would start to appear as well as the principal reduction, tax savings, appreciation etc. Few investors can handle a negative gear as it greatly raises risk and is exasperated in any potential decline. High wage earners with guaranteed income could utilize this strategy and with the normal holding period of 5 to 10 years, the property should be well on its way to providing consistent monthly cash flow plus the added bonus of an excellent capital gain (the very compelling price!), tax savings, and probably very little rental competition.

FIX and FLIPS

Whole books are written about this sub-market and popular TV Shows entice the viewer to "Get Rich". Obviously an extremely profitable undertaking when executed properly. In my search for properties, I very often encounter many opportunities to update buildings in good growth areas. There is a skill in knowing what needs to be done to update a property, the cost of the update, how long it will take to complete the project, what it will sell for, and how long the marketing time frame. Mis-read the information, and a sizable profit can turn into a loss. With experience, profits can be generated on a consistent basis. These are short term gains subject to Ordinary Income Tax.

Consider allowing the profits to remain in the property for more than12 months by leasing and claiming Long-term Capital Gains. One would obtain a below market property that upon re-rehabilitating would not only be valued at the higher value range, but also rent at a much higher range. Further, in updating the property, much of the future expenses are addressed in the initial build out such as new appliances, roof, window treatments, flooring, paint, etc. thereby lowering the repair escrow and the management costs of handling them. Depending on the how extensive the re-hab, work could easily extend to 4, 5, 6 months or beyond. Marketing time and closing could easily add another 60-90 days and the threshold for Long Term Gains could be easily within reach. A short-term tenancy could be perfect!

STUDENT HOUSING

Put away images of John Belushi in Animal House! Colleges and Universities offer opportunities to receive a premium rent roll by leasing by the bedroom rather than the unit. Hence a four bedroom house in close proximity to the school can command a generous bonus if leased to seasonal students rather than local families. Because of the general scarcity of properties, Students are often forced to lease annually through the summer alleviating much of the vacancy for the Investor. Further, usually one of the students is the main lease holder with his or her parent(s) co-signing. This simple act of additional liability helps to maintain order and allows for a chain of fiscal responsibility. Maintenance and repair is generally much higher as students are typically inexperienced with upkeep and are much harder on the premises. However, the premium received is well worth the consideration. Management needs to be assertive and clear as these are inexperienced tenants often away from home for the first time. As with any property, a guideline of expectations is very valuable.

PRIVATE PLACEMENT OFFERINGS

These are the definitions of Private Placement Offerings:

The sale of securities, real estate, or other assets to a relatively small number of select investors as a way of raising capital. Investors involved in private placements are usually large banks, mutual funds, insurance companies and pension funds. Private placement is the opposite of a public issue, in which securities are made available for sale on the open market.(investopedia.com)

Private Placements in Real Estate may also be to a much smaller investor, but usually a "Qualified" investor, meaning one that typically has $1 Million dollars in assets outside of their home. This can be changed depending on the sophistication of the buyer, but is meant to include only those that are able to assess risks and rewards at a much more astute level. This is used by many LLC's which by there nature limit the participants and allow for great flexibility in drafting terms.

Although there are as many variations as there are LLC'c, the two main groups that I currently work with are raising money for Income Properties. Typically the returns will vary depending upon the properties held, but a 6-8% annual cash return is expected usually paid quarterly plus an annual bonus of 60-70% of revenue collected beyond the contracted rate, and a negotiated 60-70% of the Capital Gain received at the end of the holding period which again varies, but is usually 5-10 years. Locally, several hotels have been packaged just blocks from the new Casino...all enormous CASH COWS!!!

This is Passive Income. A General partner is actively managing the funds and the properties. Depending on the negotiated terms and the properties held, usually the General Partner is entitled to 30-40% of the revenue generated above the guaranteed rate (6-8% in 2015) and 60-70% of the Capital Gains, A good manager is EXTREMELY valuable and one you never want to leave! In good markets, the PPO's are very difficult to enter because the rollover rate for existing Investors is so high.

The Doctrine of Enough

Y ou will become Wealthy with this strategy. I have used the Strategy, many of my friends have used the Strategy, clients and associates have used it, and ALL have done extremely well. It will create Income that comes in monthly and it GROWS and GROWS! The goal for myself has always been to prioritize what was important in my Life. My wife, my family, my faith and community, the ability to more than adequately provide for them, as well as enjoy their company free from the pressure of Life's daily expenses was always my goal. I worked very hard and created enough Wealth to provide; then reaped the rewards. It takes about 10 years for the Strategy to Season and start to provide meaningful cash flow. Obviously, depending on the entry point in any particular cycle, as well as one's ability to direct Capital into the Strategy will determine the time frame until one is "Free" and receiving Income equal to or greater than one's monthly bills. Just Do It! The sooner the better.

Let me make an observation.

So many good things happen when a young adult is allowed to remain within the Family Home. Yes, there is a maturity and responsibility factor for living outside of the home, but that also can easily be fostered within the home. Hopefully by the time your children are in their early 20's, they have watched and learned. However, consider what happens when a child stays home. Rent is automatically saved, (living cheap in a group home: $800/mn?), utilities are saved ($200), food eaten at home (we have two refrigerators and a freezer that are constantly re-stocked $400?), how about Cable, Internet, discount for bundled Car Insurance, and so many incidentals like throat lozenges, band aids, car jacks, etc that we take for granted but are certainly an expense that can alleviated by spending a limited time at home SAVING! Easily $2000 per month

every month just in fixed expenses; $25-30,000 per year. Curiously, it is just about what is needed for an Investment Property.

Every year a working adult living at home could result in a cash flowing rental. Imagine your child starting their first serious job, around 22, living at home and purchasing a rental every year until they marry. Can you imagine the life they could lead as these Income Properties really start to mature in 5+years. At 30, your children could **each** have 5-7 cash flowing rental properties already in the mature phase! Think of how that would affect their lives; instead of $40, 50, 80, 100,000 in debt with loan payments they would have Income for **LIFE!!** I am very proud of a young man I have had the privilege to know who at the age of 25 already has one free and clear rental, owns a second, and is getting ready for his third. He will not be bogged down by the mundane, but will be able to lead an Incredible Life just by this very, very simple Strategy.

Family partnerships are a good way to get started: parents-child, child-child, etc. More bonding and an excellent opportunity to reinforce good business practices such as accounting, marketing, project management, and let's not forget PEOPLE SKILLS!!! Any funds left over from school would be ideal Seed Capital. I know I will get e-mails for this, but every child does not need Harvard! Most of us are not going to Cure Cancer! Consider the wonderful Community College system across the US that delivers excellent education at very affordable prices and then transferring to a school to finish. Limit the expense. Your child can live at Home (it is and always will be thought of as Home) and commute while working part time.

I remember that age. I strongly believe we are their guides and that is why they chose us for parents. If patience can be applied for just a short time, their lives will be changed for the better, their children's lives, and for generations following.

This is an extremely successful Strategy, for me it was just a Means to an End and once the Goal was reached, **we** as a Family enjoyed the benefits. My Life just keeps getting better and better. For some there is never enough and there are some incredibly Wealthy rich people who are successful at making money yet are incredibly unhappy and unsuccessful at being human beings.

Where to Find Financing? Which Type?

T his Strategy is written for the Investor typically in the 1st Plateau of Wealth which is generally considered under $3 million. As such, the Financing currently recommended in 2015 is the boring 30 year fixed rate fully amortized home loan. It is so easy to obtain and has no pre-payment penalty. The standard home loan can be personally adjusted countless times to add to the principal reduction in good times and the additional principal reduction can be removed if times get tough. Mortgage rates are at Historical lows as in **they probably will not go any lower** and should be considered on every transaction. The Lenders are very comfortable with Residential Loans; they can be bundled and sold in the Secondary Markets. Typically, Mortgage Brokers rather than your Bank (like Chase, BofA, Wells Fargo, etc are captive lenders even though they are huge wholesale lenders) are able to shop for the very best rate. However, rates are quoted basically Nationally and the cost differences will be found in the "Garbage Fees" of Appraisal, Document Prep, Underwriting, Origination, etc. and any discounts the brokers are willing to give.

The benefits of judicial leverage are discussed elsewhere, but are are huge. At any age, the recommendation is to continue accumulating even after retiring. The long term benefits of rates at this level are extremely compelling. Usually a minimum of 20% down payment and a loan of the difference is the minimum a lender will allow. In my opinion, although the current Real Estate Bull Market is still in it's infancy having re-emerged in the 2010-2011 time frame, a Correction is due and will probably coincide with the

Global Downturn which may start in the 2015-2016 time frame. I would recommend a very conservative use of no more than 60- 65% Loan-to-value (LTV) for a safety factor and still give the benefits of leverage. **LOAD UP THE TRUCK WITH DEBT**, but watch the LTV.

Finding Tenants

T oo easy! Tenants are plentiful and more and more are entering the market every day! I have never encountered a property I could not lease and the very few that took longer than 30 days were definitely someones FAULT!! My fault! I asked too much and the market said NO! I did not like that answer, but always, always, always the market provides and if you ask the right amount it will rent. You cannot get rent for yesterday so the sooner the property rents, the sooner the revenue starts.

As part of the search for rentals, I use data from within the Universes of Properties I am most familiar with. I know at what prices other similar properties have been bought and sold. I know at what other monthly rates comparable rentals have been leased. I am armed with the knowledge of comparable rentals ranges such as my typical 3 bedroom 2 bath, 2 car garage with a fenced back yard renting $1200-1400. On a new acquisition, the initial rent becomes the baseline from which monthly rates can be adjusted for market conditions as leases expire and re-new. For the very first tenant, I am dependent on other similar properties. I price the property competitively and adjust quickly if I feel the activity is too low. Usually within a few days of acquisition or roll over, the clean up has been finished and marketing is ready to start.

I will review the premise and be sure the side walks have been swept, the grass has been cut, watered, trimmed, any landscape has been tidied and cleaned, no weeds or litter. I will be sure the front door is freshly painted, the screen door clean and squeak free. The carpets should all be freshly cleaned as well as the windows which a have the blinds open! The paint should all have been freshly touched up and the entire interior has been cleaned with particular attention to the baths and kitchen. As much as possible the property should look like a new model home that had just been detailed. I find by thoroughly cleaning the rental, I can easily receive an extra $50-100 per month.....every month! This is the time to get value add for the length of the tenancy.

I utilize every source available to find a tenant as quickly as possible and a tenant that wants to move in as soon as possible. The rental market has been very good and my forecast is for continuing high occupancy for the foreseeable future. Many tenants are found just by a simple sign prominently displayed in the yard or window. Upon acquisition, during the closing process, or upon notification to vacate from the current tenant, I will place a clean sign. Probably better than 70% of my tenants are found by this very simple method. Another very easy source are the myriad of Real Estate sites such as Zillow, Trulia, Redfin, and Craig's List. I also always recommend the services of a good Real Estate Broker who can lease the property quickly. I find the speed of leasing vastly reduces the vacancy factor which goes a long way to paying for the services of the Broker. Also, typically tenants will lease beyond the terms of the first lease term and usually re-renewal fees are discounted or non-existent.

I generally have a tenant(s) interested rather quickly and the next step is the selection process. These prospects are not looking to buy, are generally considering renting to be short term (although every long term tenant usually thinks the same, most tenants lease beyond their first year), and need to be qualified first.

My interest is to end the vacancy period as quickly as possible and all things being equal, I will negotiate toward that end. Usually there is not great price negotiation nor a list or requirements from prospective tenants; the tenant is typically more concerned with qualifying and being approved. Tenants are not buying so my thought is the requirements can be relaxed to be a little less than say FHA minimums of Income and Credit Score. Tenants (not Landlords) can offer Security deposits to be negotiated higher to mitigate any credit shortfalls. I use an application that I have designed over the years and recently updated to include e-mail address, cell contact, etc. beyond the typical references. I use the services of a very good, online Tenant Screening services which includes not only a rental credit score, but also a Criminal and Judicial Background check which the tenant pays through a credit and application fee.

If all is acceptable, I draft a lease which I have used for decades. Here in Arizona, The Landlord -Tenant Act is very clear as to the duties of both parties and should a tenant fail to pay rent, most with a very few exceptions, are ordered out by the last week of the first month. Rent is due on the 1st and is late the 2nd, as a policy, I serve notice no later than the third of the month. Sorry, I digressed! There are many lease forms available and each State has their practices; check with your Real Estate Broker or legal counsel. Here in Arizona, the security deposit can be no more than 1.5 times the rent, typically, I accept only 1 times the rent which is not to be confused with the last months rent; I have found that is generally acceptable and adequate. I also charge a cleaning fee and a pet fee if you allow pets. I have found almost 50% of my tenants will have a pet so I might as well get compensated. I am also in the process of including a clear list of charges should the lease need to be broken by the tenant. I may not include the list with the lease, but may use it as an Addendum because as we all know: "Life Happens".

The tenant always signs the lease first and returns the lease with Earnest Money in the form of a Cashier or Bank Check. After reviewing, the lease is signed and everyone is given a copy. E-mailing additional copies leaves a very nice paper trail. Upon move in, the balance is due in certified funds and a fresh key from a changed lock is passed with directions to turn on utilities, all contact numbers including emergency and after hour procedures. This last step I actually leave to my Management Company.

Select a Management Company

E veryone needs to make a profit. My vendors need to understand that I am in Business to earn a profit and want to be treated fairly, promptly, and I want to be appreciated. My vendors are in business to do the same and although I want as good a price as possible, I also want fast service if the A/C goes bad or I have a leak. So it is a two-way street. I have had many of the same vendors for a very long time; a few over a decade!

My managers are worth their weight in GOLD! My managers have been with me for well over two decades. Together we have established clear policies for the portfolio and they are the Landlords, I just own properties. They handle all of the day to day issues, collect rents, handle and oversee repairs and improvements, pay the bills, check tenants out and walk tenants in, I seldom receive a call about a problem unless it is a major repair, and most importantly: they send me a check every month!!!! They charge a fee on the low end of the fee spectrum and we have had a very good Symbiotic relationship for years. They are very aware of my need to maintain properties, but also maximize returns. They are always very conscious of whose side they service and have proven to be true Fiduciaries. Good people are very hard to find; however, they can be found all across America and when you find them: KEEP THEM!

Family is Forever, Your Cash is Not!! Generational Wealth and Family Office

This Strategy once implemented and allowed to grow will never be depleted! It will Never run out! As I age, I will continue adding to the portfolio and growing the cash flow; a Family Office will be opened to create a Generational Legacy. As your children mature, the Strategy should be available to them on a partnership basis to help with the initial cash component and guidance. After a few initial properties, they will be doing just fine! Imagine a 30 year old with 4-6 cash flowing rental properties. Just purchasing 1 additional rental every year and like Magic, 30-40 properties could easily be accumulated long before traditional retirement age. Life would be incredibly different with guaranteed Income. Living well within ones means with Income for Life removes so many of Life's constant stresses.

Consider purchasing a vacation home(s) that can be used by all Family Members. Imagine a Condo or home in Hawaii, San Diego, Miami, Broadbeach, Queensland, London, or Paris that could be used by Family Members. As everyone's properties season, more vacation homes could be added. These are meant to remain within the Family forever, so choose wisely.

Removing the need to be employed allows for contemplation of what is truly important in one's life. Everyone has an innate overriding Talent and Drive; the Strategy is meant to allow for endeavors that are personally rewarding, but may be fiscal disappointments. The Income generated is meant to be spent, the

Capital is never, ever, to be spent and is considered the Wealth of Generations to come to be used for the betterment of the Family. I do not wish to be a proponent of laziness, but rather a proponent for doing what God sent you here to do and still live well. The Strategy will remove the need for Income and hopefully remove Greed from behavior. I actually have a dream of politicians who remember the first three words of the Constitution: WE THE PEOPLE. A reminder that all power flows from those governed; for the benefit of the people not the benefit of Politicians......again I digress!!

1031 Exchanges vs Traditional Sales

I ncome Real Estate is a long term Investment meant to consistently deliver dependable cash flow month after month, year after year. The time horizon for virtually all Real Estate Investments is a minimum of 5 years and often much longer for entities as Pension Funds and Insurance Companies. Theses entities look significantly longer with some at 20 years or longer attempting to match Income requirements with Obligations. However, there are times when it becomes necessary to sell the property. This can be a result of better opportunities, the expiration of the depreciation schedule (27.5 years), or the cyclic change in the community affecting the rate of appreciation and rental revenue which may have entered the decline phase.

Selling a Property is a reasonably expensive task and not to be taken lightly. The property is taken out of production for typically months, the cost of sales, closing, and re-financing greatly impact the ROI. However, a portfolio property may have earned 20 years of appreciation and carries a large gain for an enormous profit. Here is a personal property that became fully depreciated and needed to be changed. This is rounded to better illustrate.

XXXX Cul-De-Sac

Purchased 03/1994	$62,500	
Sold 04/2014	$161,000	
Gain	$98,500 @ 20% = Tax Liability =	$19,700
Fully depreciated recapture	$48,500 @ 25% = Recapture =	$12,125
Medicare Surcharge	$98,500 @ 3.8% =	= $ 3743
Total Tax Liability		$35,568

The use of a 1031 Tax Deferred Exchange will allow the property to be sold (Exchanged) and another property purchased (Replaced), the depreciation clock re-set, and the Tax Liability Deferred by following very simple rules.

Contract language disclosing the intention to utilize IRC Section 1031 should be incorporated into any agreement: very similar wording is used for the Purchase and Sale;

"Buyer is aware that the seller may intend to perform an IRC Section 1031 tax deferred exchange. Seller requests Buyer's cooperation and agrees to hold Buyer harmless from any and all claims, delays, or liabilities resulting from such an exchange." In today's market, it is a very good idea to also disclose that the property will be assigned by the Seller. This assignment is to the Exchange Company with simple verbiage "Seller intends to assign this agreement."

For the Purchase: "Seller is aware buyer may intend to perform an IRC Section 1031 tax deferred exchange. Buyer requests seller's cooperation and agrees to hold the Seller harmless from any and all claims, delays, or liabilities resulting from such an exchange. Again, disclosure that the Agreement will be assigned is highly recommended: "Buyer intends to assign the Agreement".

The Rules are very straightforward and set in Stone!!!! There is no wiggle room on time frames! These are simplified, but a 1031 Exchange is extremely easy.

Purchase a "Like for Like" property of equal to or greater value. This is very flexible and allows for many types of properties.

All of the Proceeds must be used in the acquisition; any remaining is considered "Boot" and is taxed. No cash is to be withdrawn from the transaction.

The Property must be acquired with as much or greater debt. If the property relinquished had a loan, an equal to or greater loan should be used. This is straightforward. If a property was sold for $150,000 with a $75,000 loan, a property of equal to or greater value must be purchased. There is $75,000 in Capital that is being reinvested. The Cash in the transaction is $75,000, it will support a purchase of $225,000 with a 30% down payment and raising the

Loan amount to $150,000. Thereby re-adjusting the depreciation and adding to the tax savings, re-starting the Financing Strategy, and controlling more assets. All by deferring the Tax.

Time frames are very strict. Calendar days are used not business days. After the Relinquished Property's sale, any property that may be acquired needs to be "Identified" within 45 days. The identifying is handled with the Exchange Company; no identification, no exchange.

The identified property needs to be closed within 180 days of the sale of the "Relinquished" property or …...no exchange.

The decision to Exchange is easy.

IRC Section 1031 states:

"No gain or loss shall be recognized on the exchange of property held for productive use in a trade or business or for investment, if such property is exchanged solely for property of like-kind which is to be held either for productive use in a trade or business or for investment."

So easy. If the property is held until death, the heirs receive the property at a "Stepped Up" Basis and the Capital Gains may **all** be forgiven!! How can you not follow this Strategy????

Conclusion: The Best Real Estate Bull Market in My Lifetime is Coming!

E verything in Life cycles: Night becomes Day, Spring becomes Summer which becomes Fall which becomes Winter which becomes Spring. There is a predictability to the rhythm. There is not an exactness in larger cycles such as when the first snow will fall, but we all know that late in the cycle, Winter will come and the snow will fall. In the Business Cycle, there is also a rhythm, a cycle that stretches back thousands of years. A certain predictability that has not been completely fine tuned, but nonetheless certainly exists and a Wise Investor makes plans accordingly. It may be time to discuss an Exit Strategy from the Equity Markets with your Adviser(s). Consider the Economic Cycles.

The Equity Markets of the world appear to cycle on a 7 year pattern:

1973: Oil Embargo and start of the 1973-1974 Recession, January 1973 to December 1974 DJIA loses 46%.

1980: The start of the destructive double-dip Recession.

1987: Black Monday and the Stock Market Crash: The New Zealand Stock Market loses 60%, Stock Markets in Hong Kong fell 45.5%, Australia 41.8%, Spain 31%, the United Kingdom 26%, the United States 22%, and Canada 22.%.

1994: Bond Market Collapse: the 30 year bond rates rise 200 basis points in 9 months, Mexico Crisis, and Orange County Bankruptcy. Turbulence in the DJIA. Valley National Bank in Phoenix absorbs huge losses from Mexican Sovereign Bonds leading to the eventual demise of the Bank.

2001: NASDAQ bubble bursts. September 17th, 2001 Stock market crash; largest one day loss in DJIA. NASDAQ eventually drops from 5132 to 1148, a 78.4% loss.

2008: Start of the "Great Recession", collapse of the Real Estate Bubble, Bankruptcy of Lehman Brothers. Stock market declines; September 17th: -684.81 points, -7.13%, September 29th largest one day loss in the DJIA -777.68 points, -6.98%, October 09, 2008, – 678.91 or -7.38%, October 15, 2008, -733.08, and December 01,2008, - 679.95 or – 7.7.%

2015: Bubbles, Bubbles everywhere. Shanghai is in a parabolic spike, the German DAX is starting to break down, our own US Equities are in holding pattern. The Global Bond Bubble is at risk of implosion with any rise in interest rates. Prudence may dictate taking profits and reducing exposure to markets that may already be over valued and unsustainable.

Any Stock and Bond portfolio should be reviewed and should be designated a source of funds for re-allocation; up to 50% should be considered for tangible asset classes like Commodities, Energy, and Income Producing Real Estate. Current financing for Real Estate is especially compelling and should be originated on all properties; the loan-to-value ratios need to be conservative. With rates at historic lows, be a Borrower, not a Lender. Further in a significant downturn, long term financing may be curtailed and not available. This financing advantage will certainly be significant in the outlying years.

Unlike Securities, by contrast, the Real Estate Market is on a much longer cycle as researched by economist Homer Hoyt and Fred E. *Foldvary. An 18 year cycle of expansion to contraction appears to be evident. This is the chart from Fred E. Foldvary:*

The Great 18-Year Real Estate Cycle

Peaks in Land Value Cycle	Interval (years)	Peaks in Construction Cycle	Interval (years)	Peaks in Business Cycle	Interval (years)
1818	-	-	-	1819	-
1836	18	1836	-	1837	18
1854	18	1856	20	1857	20
1872	18	1871	15	1873	16
1890	18	1892	21	1893	20
1907	17	1909	17	1918	25
1925	18	1925	16	1929	11
1973	48	1972	47	1973	44
1979	6	1978	6	1980	7
1989	10	1986	8	1990	10
2006	17	2006	20	December 2007	18

Source: Fred E. Foldvary. *The Depression of 2008.* Berkeley: The Gutenberg Press, 2007.

All can agree 2008 marked the bursting of the Real Estate Bubble. Prices tumbled and the Cycle was reset. The Real Estate Cycle is not exact and there can be a flexibility to the time frames. However, one thing is pretty straightforward, whether it is a meager 14 years, a 20 year, or exactly an 18 year Cycle, the top of the next Cycle, which I expect will also be a huge bubble, is not due until 2022 thru 2028. My Crystal Ball predicts 2024-2026 as the peak. Plenty of time to season Investments and raise Capital again by selling any Marginal Properties.

The Strategy until 2018 will be very conservative as the Stock and Bond Markets of the entire Globe seem to be over valued, unsustainable, and very long in the tooth. I expect a severe corrections driving Money out of Securities and into Real Assets such as Commodities, Agriculture, Energy, and Real Estate. I expect the Bond Market and Stock Markets to decline precipitously as the World resets the Mal-investment of the last decade. Investments in Stocks and Bonds have done exceptionally well and re-allocating 50% into other classes may be timely. Up to 35-50% of the Capital raised can be deployed immediately to capture quality properties that Cash Flow. The need for dependable cash flow will guide the acquisitions. These properties will be exceedingly important during any downturn for their revenue generation. Properties purchased should be financed with 30 year fully amortized fixed rate mortgages, but conservatively leveraged. I am predicting these Historically low rates should rise significantly and mortgages originated now will be a huge advantage in the near future.

The Strategy for the 2018 to 2020 time frame will be one of adding properties of opportunity to the cash flowing portfolio. Economic Turmoil will cloud Investor's judgment and fear may cause mis-givings should a major Recession cause Economic Distress. This will be a **Buying Opportunity** when prices start to stabilize about 18 months after the recognized onset of the downtrend. I have experienced the 1973-1974 Recession, the 1980-1982 double-dip recession, the 1990-1992 Recession, the 2001-2002 Recession, and the Grandaddy of them all, the 2008-2010 Great Recession. The worst mistakes I made was believing the uptrend would last much longer than it actually did and not culling marginal properties to raise cash. The number one mistake was giving in to fear and definitely not buying enough when the Properties were on a Clearance Sale. I believe another major Recession is in the works. If I am wrong, the Properties will still Cash Flow and add to the Income Revenue. If I am right, they will supplement and/or sustain the cash flow needs in an Economic Downturn. The Strategy works in both scenarios.

In the Summer of 2015, the Equities Markets may be approaching a Cycle Top; while the Real Estate Cycle appears to be approaching only a correction in a much longer Cycle. Re-allocating a portion of the Stock and Bond funds to Real Estate seems to be a reasonable and prudent course of action. As for the longer Real Estate Cycle, there are many reasons for a continuing Bull Market in Real Estate.

The Baby Boomer" generation has affected every market they demographically encountered: from elementary schools to muscle cars and now retirement activities. The new generation of "Millennials" are set to **surpass** the "Boomers". They have affected

Universities and tuition costs; soon they will marry and form families of their own again increasing the demand for homes with a yard and space for a swing set. The Cycle for Financial Assets is coming to a close and the Cycle for Real Assets is continuing and will gain momentum. A portfolio of oil, coal, lumber, agriculture, precious metals, and of course Real Estate will be favored over Financial Assets. Deflation will give way to Inflation as years of ZIRP (Zero Interest Rate Policy) finally affect the Economy. When the Recession appears, mal-investments will be cleared bringing turmoil to marginal assets creating opportunities. Conditions such as these are extremely favorable for Hard Assets and Income Producing Real Estate.

Let me again refer to the Phases of a Bubble Chart by Dr. Jean Paul Rodrigue and the cycle sign posts

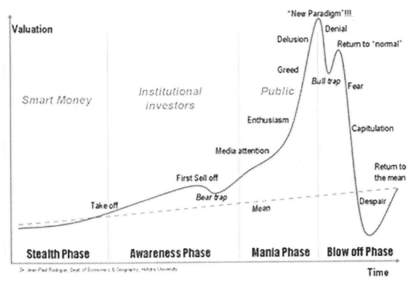

Phases of an asset bubble

The 2015 Real Estate market should be approaching the First Sell Off which can be viewed as a correction in an ongoing Bull Market. Better pricing typically is available when the turmoil from the Global Economy causes a Recession. However, in a Recession, financing may be curtailed or much more expensive. A portion of re-allocated funds should be used to capture cash flowing properties and current compelling long term rates used for the acquisition. The cash generated by these properties will be a life line in an Economic tempest. Before the ending of the current cycle, which I expect in the 2024-2026 time frame, I expect prices to be **very significantly higher.** Should a Global slowdown manifest in the next few years, it will be a Generational buying opportunity. The Greatest Real Estate Bull Market in my Lifetime is still before me. Within 5 years, Fortunes will be Lost and Fortunes Made; Cash Flowing Income Properties will create Wealth for Generations to come.

The End

Appendix

Thanks for use of the graph and data on page 5 of the:

The Depression of 2008
by Fred E. Foldvary
Second edition, Sept. 18, 2007
Copyright 2007. All rights reserved.
Permission to copy excerpts for publication is granted provided
that full credit (author, year, title, publisher, page numbers) is given
and a
copy of the publication is sent to the Gutenberg Press.
ISBN 0-9603872-0-X
The Gutenberg Press
PO Box 9597
Berkeley CA 94709
gutenbergpress@pobox.com

Thanks to Dr. Jean Paul Rodrigue for the Phases of a Bubble Chart.

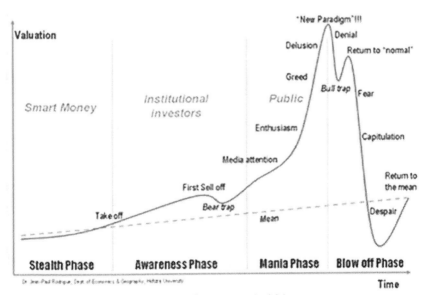

Phases of an asset bubble

About the Author

Mr. Douville has been in the Real Estate Business since 1974, over 41 years. He started his career during the 1974 recession in the Southwest suburbs of Chicago, where he experienced an inflationary period followed by the crash.

In 1981, having experienced enough cold and snow, he and his wife of now almost 36 years moved to beautiful Scottsdale, Arizona. For the last 34 years, Mr. Douville has advised clients, coached Basketball at the YMCA and Boys Club, participated in innumerable Boy Scout outings, and played Golf three times.

From 1982 through the early 1990's, the Douville's executed their well-thought-out business plan to accumulate income producing single family homes; the strategy has now been published. Michael currently represents and consults with investors for Aquisition, Wealth Management, and Asset Preservation while overseeing a portfolio of investment properties.

Michael has travelled with his family extensively within Australia and New Zealand, has journeyed on numerous occasions to the South Pacific, Europe, Mexico, Canada and the Caribbean, and of course throughout the US

Made in the USA
Middletown, DE
30 August 2017